MATTERS OF DIRT AND LEATHER

a walk through the beatitudes

BETHANN MILLER

illustrations by Kate Saurman

b.a. perspectives

Contact the author: safeplaceministry.org

Cover and interior illustrations by Kate Saurman
Prayers by Amy Beth Velarde
Editing by Elizabeth Trotter (storiessetfree.com)
Cover and interior design by Lisa Von De Linde (lisavdesigns.com)
Author photo of Bethann Miller by Christopher Dean

Paperback ISBN: 979-8-218-77062-4

First Edition, 2025
Printed in the United States of America

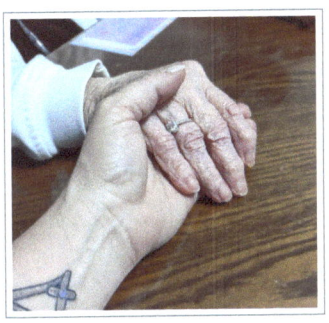

Dedicated to my Mom, 1936–2022

Thanks for always encouraging me to share
my five loaves and two fish

TABLE OF CONTENTS

FOREWORD

I first encountered Bethann at a profound crossroads in my own life—a time filled with questions, grief, and the slow work of learning to let go. Bethann met me in that season with what I can only describe as the language of the Kingdom. It was a way of seeing, naming, and honoring what lies beneath the surface—where our wounds and our hopes dwell side by side.

The language of the Kingdom is wholly unlike the language of the world's power structures. In a world that prizes strength, self-reliance, and image—qualities I myself can cling to—Bethann quietly modeled something different. Her presence conveyed the language of dirt rather than leather: humility, honesty, and the willingness to bear witness to pain without being consumed by it.

As I began to understand this language for myself, it became clear how easily the world's systems those rooted in self-advancement and control—can infiltrate even our churches and ministries. Sometimes, perhaps especially so.

As we continued our conversations, I discovered that Bethann and I were both drawn to the teachings of Jesus in the Sermon on the Mount. Of all the Scriptures, Matthew 5-7 is the passage I find myself returning to most often. The Beatitudes, in particular, have become for me a kind of compass—a set of signposts pointing toward a different way of being that too often gets overlooked in our race for success, influence, and security.

Bethann's presence conveyed the language of dirt rather than leather: humility, honesty, and the willingness to bear witness to pain without being consumed by it.

Many before us have lingered here in Jesus' profound messaging, soaking in these words and letting them do the slow work of transformation. St. Augustine of Hippo wrote, "The Beatitudes are arranged in a perfect order: for there is none more perfect than this order, which begins with humility." In more recent times, Mother Teresa captured their essence when she said, "The Beatitudes are everything. If we live them, we live the gospel."

This ancient path isn't about right doctrine alone or a checklist of behaviors; it is an invitation to live differently and was signposted years before by the prophet Micah: "Do justice, love mercy, and walk humbly with your God."

The real question is—how do we embody this posture? How do we walk it out in our families, communities, faith institutions, and workplaces—especially when power tempts us to drift from humility and mercy? In Jesus, we see the pattern lived out: He moved through the corridors of power not with domination, but with meekness. He entered into the world's suffering, not above it but beside it, and He called His followers to the same.

Bethann's devotional, *Matters of Dirt and Leather,* is not merely a guide for intellectual exploration—though it certainly holds much to ponder. It is, above all, a gentle invitation: to sit at the feet of Christ, to slow down, reflect, and let His words work their quiet revolution in you. As you read, I encourage you to linger in the questions, allow your heart to be unsettled, and give yourself permission to wrestle with what is uncomfortable. In this, the Spirit will teach us the language of the Kingdom. It is nothing less than learning to follow Jesus and embody justice, mercy, and radical humility in a world that desperately needs all three.

Welcome to the beautiful journey of dirt and leather.

Donovan Palmer

CEO, Mission Aviation Fellowship International

Matters of Dirt and Leather

INTRODUCTION

Dirt is gritty, sometimes messy. It can hold, nurture, and provide food. Children and even adults enjoy playing in it and connecting to creation in a life-giving way.

Leather is the result of death. It is meant to cover and represents a strong exterior. Tough and often worn by folks who seem powerful, it is also connected to creation. Leather comes from dirt and one day will return to that form, as it is derived from the skin of animals.

In this book we will be looking at the Beatitudes through the lens of systems of power (leather) and the teachings of Christ (dirt) in a time when they were largely misrepresented—the time of the Roman Empire and the life of Jesus Christ. We will see what we can learn and apply today in a season of abuse of power in our churches, societies, and political platforms.

This book is meant to be used as a devotional of sorts. I have left the chapters intentionally short to engage your intellect, heart, and soul. I invite you to take time with it. Contemplate the scriptural text. Let your thoughts be challenged and belief systems explored.

The artwork was created by Kate Saurman. She captured what I had seen in my mind and translated it into beautiful and thought-provoking images. Let them also challenge you. The Beatitudes are commonly depicted in fluffy or flannel graph Sunday School art, but in reality they are some of the most difficult teachings Christ ever gave. So take the time to consider the images as you engage with each chapter. (Kate is an artist and advocate serving marginalized populations in Brazil.)

Thank you for taking this little journey with me. It is my hope that we are each challenged, encouraged, and changed to represent Christ in a world that desperately needs hope and life as we use and hold our power carefully.

Blessed are the poor in spirit,
for theirs is the kingdom of heaven.

Blessed are those who mourn,
for they will be comforted.

Blessed are the meek,
for they will inherit the earth.

Blessed are those who hunger and
thirst for righteousness,
for they will be filled.

Blessed are the merciful,
for they will be shown mercy.

Blessed are the pure in heart,
for they will see God.

Blessed are the peacemakers,
for they will be called children of God.

Blessed are those who are persecuted
for the sake of righteousness,
for theirs is the kingdom of heaven.

MATTHEW 5:3-10

A NOTE FROM THE ARTIST

When Bethann contacted me about illustrating the Beatitudes, I did not have a framework for what she would write to fill each chapter. I was given the biblical imagery she chose to accompany the verses and asked to create a small black-and-white ink drawing for each.

I began working on the outlines as she requested, but they did not seem to convey the full story. Each Beatitude, although already perfect when written centuries ago, is still evolving within the structure of our lives. These teachings, what some say are the points of Jesus' inaugural address, are molding us, maturing us as we not only meditate on them, but apply them; they are an ongoing formation of Christ within each Christian. They are how we model heaven on earth, and yet not one of us has arrived at a finished state to say what that looks like. So how could they be drawn?

The black-and-white drawings that I had begun constructing felt very two-dimensional. They lacked the uncertainty of what was being formed— the choices, the character development, the mess that these verses prepare us to walk through. Exploring this tension, between ideas with solid definition and deeply nuanced personal challenges to "work them out in the flesh," I decided to play with some watercolor.

Ink lines are a form of media that allow for high levels of control, but painting in watercolor often feels like an act of surrender. There is movement, there is error, there is possibility, and there is an invitation to partner with the one who created water and color itself—not knowing what the final result will look like.

In a way, the acts of filling these ink outlines with running color served as a reminder that perfection is found only in and through Christ. As we pursue Him even within the dichotomies that test and refine our understanding, He makes our childlike efforts into reflections of His truth. He is not afraid of the mess but offers to meet us there.

Kate Saurman
Artist

OPENING PRAYER

Father, we come to You as we begin this journey of learning through Your son Jesus' teachings. In a world in which our constructs and systems are so broken, in which misuse of power and position often hurt rather than help the precious ones You created, You have come near and shown us a more excellent way (1 Cor. 12:31).

Jesus, You flipped the tables and the scripts and showed us what You value and will bless. Your kingdom is so unlike this world, so opposite of what we've been taught and the way our finite minds naturally think. Please expand our minds and hearts to see your kingdom in all its beauty, mystery, and glory. Challenge our small thinking and living. Stir in us a holy discontent with this world. May Your words and teachings transform us so we may shine like stars as we hold out the word of hope to this watching world (Phil. 2:16).

Amen.

AMY BETH VELARDE

Blessed are the poor in spirit;

For theirs is the kingdom
of heaven.

Matthew 5 : 3

CHAPTER ONE

BLESSED
ARE THE POOR IN SPIRIT

A thorny branch was twisted and placed on the head of Jesus as He was about to walk down the Via Dolorosa, a road in the old city of Jerusalem where Christ was forced by the Roman guards to carry the wooden beams used for His crucifixion. This crown of thorns mocked the King who seemingly would not come to His own defense—and whose followers had fled in fear upon His arrest.

The leather-clad soldiers stood by and scorned Jesus, spitting on Him as He passed by with the symbol of torture saved for the worst criminals in this society—murderers, thieves, and those who plotted to overthrow the emperor.

It was not Roman rulers who placed Him there, but religious leaders who held the systems of power. The people who professed worship and piety yet used their power to inflict further suffering on the poor, crushing them with burdens of faith and exploiting an already diminished state of living. They were not wearing breastplates of leather but rather robes of power that produced death.

> The dirt of the crown of thorns invites us to a more excellent way

The leather symbolizing the Roman government, religious leaders, and power brokers leads to death. The dirt of the crown of thorns invites us to a more excellent way, a less traveled road, one that sometimes incurs suffering—and even death. In the light of these symbols, Jesus invites us to examine whose kingdom we are living for.

For those of us who desire the kingdom of heaven, Jesus instructs us to be poor in spirit. But we struggle to understand what that means. Do we need to live in constant poverty? Never having what we need, creating in us a driving dependence on God, on others, on ourselves? In my study of this through the years, I suggest a different way to look at it.

To be poor in spirit means that we know who we are, and we understand the authority we have been given. We have a willingness to live, relate, and practice governance in the value and care of others. We seek to reflect God's loving-kindness (intent for wholeness) and not engage with power in a way that exploits others. In essence, we handle power in a righteous way.

During my time living and serving overseas on a missionary hospital ship, my first position was housekeeping. I was tasked with cleaning cabins for guests and new crew members and the keeping of public areas. This would include the "heads"—aka the bathrooms on a ship.

About one month into my first tenure of service, two male crew members who decided they didn't like me maliciously smeared defecation all over the stalls of the men's room. I was hurt, furious, and confused. Why on earth would someone on a Christian missionary ship treat me like this? I went to the head of the department and abruptly announced that I would not be cleaning up their (you fill in the blank).

My manager in her direct Dutch way (shout out to all dutchies who practice direct communication) said, "Ok, Bethann, you have a choice to make. This is clearly wrong and reprehensible, and I will talk with them. I will clean it up if you want, or you can and, in this way, practice the practical expression of being poor in spirit. You do not deserve this, and it is clearly wrong. No one would blame you if you opted out."

I put my gloves on and scrubbed those toilet stalls as if I were worshiping! It was not pleasant, and I was angry. I also knew I had an opportunity to embrace the dirt of others' offense or put on the leather of injustice.

How are you and I carrying our power?

Are we entangled in a system that looks out for our own good
and "us first," or are we taking the narrow path
of humility and value of others
that looks and feels sometimes like a crown of thorns?

Blessed are those who mourn, for they will be comforted.

Matthew 5 : 4

CHAPTER TWO

BLESSED
ARE THOSE WHO MOURN

To mourn we must first be willing to receive and embrace the unwanted and uninvited companions of grief and loss.

As Christians we sometimes erroneously expect a life without suffering. When we construct a belief system that seemingly protects us from suffering, we will inevitably lack the spiritual, relational, and emotional maturity to experience the difficult situations in our lives and in the lives of those we love and care for.

Mourning doesn't seem like a blessing. It is often messy and disorienting. It is lonely and not experienced in the same way from person to person. It is a journey that sometimes will not reach its destination until we enter eternal life.

Mourning requires a certain level of integrity inside us. It requires us to live without editing any of the difficult parts out. It requires an embrace of the truth. An acceptance of our disappointment with how things should have gone or what should have happened.

So why would Christ share these odd and disruptive words with us?

Those of us in the developed world have built systems to mitigate pain and discomfort. Some of them are medicinal, some are religious belief systems of prosperity, some are made clear through advertisements luring us into yet another means of material or environmental escape. But our carefully crafted systems are stunting our own maturation process.

We look to the government to ensure we have as little discomfort as possible. Those of us in the USA might even categorize this desire as a basic American right. We disassociate ourselves from a very intimate part of our souls. What are we so afraid of?

Tragically, our fears and discomfort separate us from understanding and relating to a world that needs others to sit with them in their grief and to mourn alongside them.

In the nation of The Gambia, West Africa, where I was serving as a missionary, I met a young woman named Awa. She was nineteen years old and had come to the medical ship I was serving on in the hopes that doctors could help her. After being screened by a friend of mine named Sonja who was the head of the medical department, it became clear that Awa's needs were acute and too much for medical help.

She had arrived in the back of a bush taxi with her grandmother and was wrapped in what looked like grave clothes to me. As they unwrapped her head to introduce us, I was not prepared for what I would see. The tumors that had no access to medical intervention had broken both her eye sockets and protruded out in grotesque form, inviting me to a depth of human suffering I had never witnessed before. It shook me to my core.

What are we so afraid of?

Back on the deck of the hospital ship where the other missionaries and I lived, I stayed awake all through that night wrestling with God. I was rendered speechless by the profound suffering I was seeing.

I wanted to run. Run back to my clean Christian belief systems of "It's all going to be okay" and "God will not give you more than you can handle." This situation seemingly spat in the face of all those childish and underdeveloped thoughts. This was profound suffering, and I was invited into it.

Over the next few weeks, I would take friends from the ship to visit Awa and pray and read scriptures over her. Rachel, a beautiful woman from Britain, came and played her violin in Awa's room of mud and dirt to comfort and express beauty in music. We read of the "suffering servant, well acquainted with grief," so she would know that someone understood her pain.

Awa passed in a very difficult manner in the weeks following. The other crew members who joined me in visiting her were invited into something very sacred—to bear witness to another's suffering and to let our belief systems be challenged, changed, and comforted. To enter our own, or another's, suffering with impact and to experience the care and comfort only Christ can bring us.

This is where we are called blessed and comforted when we mourn.

Comforted to mourn for the loss of a family member.

Comforted to mourn the loss of justice in racial equity.

Comforted to mourn for the loss of a child.

Comforted to mourn the faulty belief system that frailly held our faith.

Comforted to mourn for the loss of a dear friend to domestic violence.

Comforted to mourn for the loss of a friendship or demise of a marriage.

Comforted to mourn the loss of a life we expected and were even taught we should expect.

Isaiah 53:3 says of the Messiah, "He was despised and rejected by mankind, a man of suffering, and familiar with pain. Like one from whom people hide their faces he was despised, and we held him in low esteem."

As you and I seek to become more Christlike in our daily lives and as we care for others, we must leave space for suffering and acceptance of various forms of hardships. Because this same Messiah who knew deep suffering also promised His followers, "Blessed are those who mourn, for they will be comforted."

In our culture and faith, we have often been instructed to mask or at the very least contain our grief and loss. To mourn requires humility and the willingness to be truly seen. It is messy and can make others around us very uncomfortable.

Living in Africa for so many years showed me a different type of grieving. When a family member dies, the women of the village gather and wail. The first time I experienced this, it was disturbing. It seemed out of control, human emotion gone amuck.

But death and suffering are a common experience in the developing world, and in my opinion, they are usually experienced with a greater fidelity to the loss. These loud and often uncomfortable expressions of grief perhaps communicate the true weight of what our souls are going through when we mourn.

If you look at your places of suffering and loss,
have they needed to be nicely contained and expressed
in a clean manner? To mourn requires vulnerability.
And it is here within this very place that Christ desires to meet us
with His comfort. How is He comforting you?

1

2

"Blessed are the meek, for they shall inherit the earth."

– Matthew 5 : 5

CHAPTER THREE

BLESSED
ARE THE MEEK

We all hope our parents and grandparents do well enough for us to receive an inheritance. But what is this inheritance based on? Money? Property? A business? A church or ministry? A good name that we cannot tarnish?

You and I inherited the family systems we were raised in. Some of these may include money, position, or even companies and ministries to lead. But family systems are usually more nuanced than monetary means. They are also the relational, financial, spiritual, sexual, and emotional systems of living that we are born into. Not all of them are based on wholeness.

We inherit political, financial, and religious views. Prejudice is often inherited and passed down to the following generations. We inherit ideas without examining them against truth. But what does meekness have to do with any of this?

Meekness means great strength under total control. This definition changes the landscape for us.

In our society today we go to great lengths not to show weakness or vulnerability. These things are considered less than. As we curate and present a social profile that communicates strength, health, and having it all together, we are all slowly dying. I know. I talk with folks for a living.

We seem to be losing the ability to control our emotions and actions. Forfeiting our self-control is seemingly the trend today. We think, "I couldn't help myself," or "The system did this to me." We are living in a victim mentality world.

We do not need to live like this. Power is often abused when there are no constraints on it. We can see this evidenced in civilizations gone by. Empires rise and fall. Governments exploit and pillage the very people they are entrusted to protect and govern. Power is fleeting and fickle.

In the fall of 2001, I led a group of forty-one people on a prayer and reconciliation walk around the nation of Northern Ireland. It took us two months to complete this journey, walking ten to eighteen miles a day, rain or shine. (Both happen beautifully there.)

The "Troubles," as they are known, were just ending. This was a time when the Irish Republican Army and the British Army were fighting against each other. It was a bloody and violent time, and it was between two expressions of Christian faith. The folks in Northern Ireland were largely Catholic, and folks from Britain were Protestant.

In the course of history there have always been religious wars and probably always will be. Humans look to impose their views on others and demand submission and loyalty through geopolitical means. The genocide in Rwanda is another well-known war that was waged between two professions of Christian faith.

> Meekness means great strength under total control. This definition changes the landscape for us.

During this trip to Northern Ireland, our long line of forty-one wet and tired folks would stay at a Catholic church and receive gracious hospitality and care one night, and then the next night a Protestant church would provide the same for us. We would worship through song in the city squares where the bombings took place and hear stories of the lives that were lost and impacted during this tumultuous time in history.

How desperately sad—and so far from the kingdom of God. Killing was not the inheritance either side wanted to hand down to their children.

On a smaller scale, when you and I choose to use our power in a way that is not controlled, we are not walking in meekness. We do damage to ourselves and others, and we take the name of the Lord in vain through our actions. Where do we need to learn how to walk in the meekness of Christ in our own lives so the inheritance we leave is one of wholeness and health and not the abuse of power?

When Christ said, "Render to Caesar the things that are Caesar's, and to God the things that are God's," He was instructing us to hold those two systems of power very separate (Mark 12:17 NASB95). One will exploit and always fall short. The other brings life and comes from God Himself: "And the government will be on His shoulders . . . of the greatness of His government and peace there will be no end" (Isa. 9:6–7).

Rulers, kings, and governments will come and go. Empires will rise and fall. These are very fragile and faulty systems of rules that we tend to put all our hope and trust in. But those systems cannot save us or usher us into the kingdom of heaven.

When we use our power to exploit for our own selfish means, we are not living in accordance with what the Lord has invited us to. But stewardship stands in opposition to exploitative power. To steward something means to carefully and responsibly manage something entrusted to our care.

So how are you and I stewarding what has been entrusted to us?
Money, time, power, relationships, creation?
In caring rightly for the things God has given us, we reveal
His glory—and we inherit the earth He made for us.

Blessed are those who hunger and thirst after righteousness,

for they shall be filled
— Matthew 5 : 6

CHAPTER FOUR

BLESSED ARE THOSE WHO HUNGER AND THIRST FOR RIGHTEOUSNESS

I was sitting in an abandoned, dirt-filled lot in New York City after a long day feeding the homeless, outcasts, and squatters who lived in and around the condemned buildings on the Lower East Side.

A man who was a squatter and who had come for food earlier in the day said to me, "Where are you squatting?"

I was in my mid-twenties at the time and serving with an urban ministry that provided food and resources to folks who lived outside. It can be difficult for people to go to shelters and programs for many reasons. We wanted to serve them exactly where they lived—outside. This came with some great challenges and ministry lessons for me as I was "green behind the ears."

On Fridays I would take a few people with me in a van to pick up food from the business kitchens at the Twin Towers (World Trade Center). We would drive in from Long Island where the ministry was located and take the freight elevators through the back hallways of the towers. The kitchen staff would be pleased to see us and load us up with unused food.

Then we would head back to Long Island to prepare all the food for the thousand-person crowd, and we would serve it, rain or shine, the next day on the streets.

At times this could be grueling work. We were serving in the elements three days a week. If someone gave us a big aggressive hug (which was probably a mix of gratitude plus whatever substance had recently been consumed), we would need to check ourselves for needlesticks at the end of the day. The cold and the heat were not adjustable. They mirrored the environments most of these precious folks were living in.

We both hungered for food, shelter, and a place of belonging.

Some of the elderly women who would come and help were squatters living in the condemned buildings outside Tompkins Square Park. One of these women was named Maria.

She was in her late seventies with a few teeth missing, which you could see when she broke into her huge smile. She was from Ukraine but had fled war in her country and had come to America for a better life. Things do not always work out how we hope or expect. But Maria was happy to be here. She would come every day we were out on the streets to help us keep the line of folks under control, as she had a bossy way about her!

Maria invited me to dinner at her home one day after we were done serving. As we walked into the abandoned building, she said in her broken English, "The steps will fall, be careful." I followed her in her skirts, multiple sweaters, and the head scarf traditional of her native country.

She seemed to move easily and without care, leading me up three floors with great holes as we climbed. No electricity, no water, no heat, but a little Sterno stove she would cook on. She served me a beautiful meal of borscht and homemade pierogies, and she told me tales of her homeland. We shared life, and she filled my belly. The ministry was giving out of excess, but Maria provided for me out of her lack and insecurity.

When this day was over, I went outside and sat down on a rock in the abandoned lot and pondered the graciousness of humanity I was experiencing. This is when the man who was squatting posed to me one of the most beautiful questions I have ever been asked: "Where are you squatting?"

I was a mess from the day of serving. Dirty, smelly, sticky, and full of stains from who knows what. His question was so welcomed, as it communicated to me that I did not appear threatening or better than he was.

I was accepted, and there was no power dynamic between us. We both hungered for food, shelter, and a place of belonging.

Many years later, my husband Tom and I lived for a week in a camp in Liberia where people who had contracted leprosy lived. These folks were banished from their villages, just like in the days that Christ taught the very scriptures we are discussing on these pages.

We were struck by the apparent and contagious joy they had. They were not looking for our pity or a remedy for the disease that had changed the course of their lives. They desired friendship, the company of others, and enjoying a meal that validated their humanity. They could endure deep suffering as long as they had the gift of community.

What are you hungering and thirsting for?
Things that numb and pull you away from experiencing life?
Money, that might you gain a false sense of control
over all the outcomes of your life? Fame or power
that leaves you empty and often with fractured relationships?
These are all poorly constructed knockoffs that lure us
into a false sense of worth. If we hunger and thirst
for righteousness—doing right by God, doing right by ourselves,
doing right by others—we will be filled.

Blessed are the
merciful, for they
will be shown
mercy.

Matthew 5 : 7

CHAPTER FIVE

BLESSED ARE THE MERCIFUL

It has been my experience with myself and walking alongside others that we desire mercy for ourselves and often judgment for others.

This shines a light on the state of our hearts. We can be in such need of something for ourselves that we often forget the kindness of God and others toward us. Mercy is not free for us, and it is not free toward others. The sufferings of Christ display this, and we can follow in a like manner.

Mercy is often depicted as weak. As we see in the image painted for this chapter, it is actually full of strength and intention. It is not flippant, nor liberal. It is first and foremost based in truth and in the intrinsic value of the person in need of it.

To acknowledge that we need someone's mercy, we must first examine ourselves and admit the transgression of whatever ordinance we have violated. We tend to carry measuring tapes for this when it comes to others but forget when it comes to ourselves.

In 1999 I was in Duncan Village, a township outside the city of East London, South Africa. This unique and beautiful country has a sad and destructive history, particularly during the turmoil and chaos of apartheid.

This institutionalized system of racial segregation affected the very fabric of the nation from the late 1940s until it ended in the mid-1990s through the endless work and suffering of Nelson Mandela and Archbishop Desmond Tutu. Even in 1999 when I visited, the impoverished township of East London was full of desperation, violence, and a profound lack of provision, safety, and perhaps most acutely, hope.

Fires would often erupt from the open-flame paraffin fuel that was used to cook or stay warm when the winter set in. When this happened and the winds rolled over the hillsides, many of the cardboard and tin shacks would go up in flames with no way to stop the devouring inferno.

There was no running water or electricity in this township. The inhabitants were Black, and during this time in South African society, this meant they held very little value in the eyes of others.

I and a crew of two hundred were docked in East London on a ship so that we could provide medical care. A few of us would travel in and out of Duncan Village every day to do CHE, or Community Health Education, in the schools and churches, and that's where I met a wonderful group of people that I soon fell in love with.

We began a daily Bible study at Selena's house that was often so crowded you could only find a place to sit on the ground. So much laughter, good conversation, and friendship was built as we explored the parables of Jesus from the Gospel of Matthew.

Xhosa was the language they spoke, and I would try with all my might to learn the deep clicks and sounds they made to accent words. I was not adept at this language, but they loved that I tried!

I had decided to sleep over at Selena's house one night to spend time with her. This caused a bit of an uproar in the community. Apparently no white person, let alone a woman, had ever spent a night in Duncan Village. It was far too dangerous. The lasting effect of the racial scarring remained.

But I was determined—I was spending the night in Selena's shack. That evening would become one of the few sacred moments in my life when the liminal space between heaven and earth seems to disappear.

When I arrived at the two-room shack, I was greeted with a bed made from rice sacks stuffed with hay, with torn bedsheets turned down at the corner. Selena explained that she used to have a job in hospitality but lost it due to her color. Yet here she was, rolling out the red carpet for me. She provided a bucket in case I needed to relieve myself in the night, as the community open-air latrines were a good distance away and far too dangerous a journey to take at night.

I had asked a friend from the ship to accompany me, and our host invited us to sit outside on buckets around a rickety wooden table and join her for a beautiful meal of some sort of sausage and vegetable.

Selena's elderly neighbor who lived in the shack adjacent to hers joined us for the meal. He was a very thin man with quiet eyes who was wearing a tee shirt with the name of a well-known brand from the USA. We laughed during the meal and shared stories about what our lives were like, simply enjoying each moment.

At the end of the meal, this quiet old man who hadn't said a word during supper gently stood up and said, "Now I know God is real. I have eaten a meal in peace with a white person." And he withdrew into his shack.

> I had the distinct feeling and clarity that heaven and earth were touching each other that night.

My friend and I were speechless. What had we just experienced? How many folks had given their lives, suffering from the ravages of injustice, so that we could have this shared moment of humanity?

We said goodnight, and Selena settled in to sleep on the dirt floor since we were her honored guests. I lay down on the bed made of rice bags stamped with USAID and WFP and heard the sound of rats scurrying above and around us (I am not fond of rats). Yet I had the distinct feeling and clarity that heaven and earth were touching each other that night. The Veil was thin and I was fully alive—a child of God.

Mercy was expressed to me in this beautiful township
where I was welcomed with open arms
and the utmost of hospitality.
Where do you and I need to serve others
generously with the gift of mercy?

Blessed are the pure in heart,
for they will see God.

Matthew 5:8

CHAPTER SIX

BLESSED
ARE THE PURE IN HEART

In a meme circulating on the internet, Winnie the Pooh sits down after a difficult day. Piglet sits down next to him, but Pooh doesn't want to talk about what's bothering him. Piglet's quiet companionship seems to make Pooh's burden a little lighter even though Piglet's presence does not change Pooh's situation.

As we look at this next Beatitude through the lens of how we steward our power and authority in Christian service, we need to consider what bearing each other's burdens means. How do we come alongside others without an agenda, power dynamic, or need to control? To me this is part of being pure in heart.

I have the honor of sitting with leaders, pastors, and missionaries every day and hearing their stories. Stories of systems that require so much out of an individual that the person in service is often taken advantage of. He or she is expected to be a servant and be "all in." This may sound good on the surface, but in the end the worker ends up feeling exploited.

These systems of ministry demand allegiance, and when someone begins to break under the weight of it all or to express an opinion that does not align with said system, they are often discarded or forced to leave. Sometimes this is done directly, but often it is through passive-aggressive leadership and groupthink.

What if we aimed at treating and responding to people with an intent for wholeness and well-being, even amid personal and ministerial failure and hardship?

This is not a reflection of coming alongside as a burden bearer, and it is one of the things Jesus spoke so directly about to the religious leaders during His time. In Matthew 23:4, Jesus said, "They crush people with unbearable religious demands and never lift a finger to ease the burden" (NLT). In contrast, Psalm 68:19 speaks of God, "who daily bears our burdens," and Galatians 6:2 instructs us to "carry each other's burdens." As the body of Christ, we need to grow and mature in this area.

In Scripture, the term "loving-kindness" has a deeper meaning of "intent for wholeness." What if we aimed at treating and responding to people with an intent for wholeness and well-being, even amid personal and ministerial failure and hardship? This approach reflects the Lord, who is pure in heart.

In my thirty-three years of active Christian service, I have learned a lot about myself, others, and systems of ministry. Most of all, I have learned and been deeply affected by God's heart for wholeness and well-being that is directed toward us as His image bearers.

At the start of my ministry career, I was serving with a ministry on the streets of New York City. I adored the folks we cared for, and they held such a special place in my heart. They were scrappy and so was I. (That is one of the highest compliments anyone can give me.) I was also very young and naive to some of the underbelly of ministry. A rude awakening was in store for me.

Being new to ministry, I was not expecting desperately unhealthy leadership, deep board dysfunction, and the unspoken command "not to touch the Lord's anointed." So many precious folks have been taught, disciplined, and crushed into silence by this awful misappropriation of scripture. Those who challenge the system are clearly the problem and often labeled rebellious. This sad fact of life almost took me out of ministry.

At first, I was convinced of what I was hearing from other staff, that the problem was all me. I was young, inexperienced in ministry, and not yet formed in the core of myself to be able to trust what I was feeling. In fact, I was told time and time again that the heart (my heart) was wicked and should not be trusted. I desired to please others, and so I agreed with the leadership. It must be me. Until it wasn't.

There were side comments about staff being difficult and needing to learn lessons. I was prohibited from entering specific parts of the facility because I couldn't be trusted. Countless times I was directed to do the tasks no one else wanted to. I grew exhausted, and my body began to show the evidence of this.

I grew increasingly agitated and anxious. I struggled to maintain clarity of thought and found myself deeply conflicted in my spirit, soul, and body. I was confused and deeply skeptical of my own heart. Maybe they were right? Maybe I was not cut out for ministry and couldn't hack it, as I had been told. Something had to give.

I remember the night I resigned from this ministry. I was sitting on a cold concrete floor in a food warehouse, sorting through spoiled dairy products—which was all I could be entrusted with. It was after 1 a.m. as I held my breath, anxiously waiting until the vans and the director of the ministry returned from their outreach that night.

As the director walked over, looking at me with such disgust in her eyes, I stood up. I handed her my keys to the ministry building and walked out. She followed me, screaming, "You will never amount to anything in ministry, and you have nothing to offer."

While leaving was a relief, the thoughts and questions in my heart and mind would haunt me for quite some time. Perhaps I was a failure and not cut out for ministry. Maybe my heart was wicked and there was no hope for me. So many difficult questions plagued me. I left alone, and painfully the colleagues I served with did not respond to my attempts at a relationship for over a year. (Eventually many of them had to leave under their own distress.)

My heart, body, and spirit were badly bruised. I was not emotionally, relationally, or spiritually healthy—many folks serving in ministry are not. But these circumstances often come with an invitation. An invitation to grow, to mature, to learn of the Burden Bearer, and to be made into His image.

I stepped out of direct ministry for a year and took a job at a low-end convenience store named, ironically enough, Rock Bottom. Stocking shelves and cutting boxes, I let the Lord heal, mature, and develop me. I would like to say that the process was completed after that year. Yet, here I am, thirty-four years later, still learning, growing, and becoming. As Henri Nouwen put it, I am a "wounded healer."

I have revisited these themes many times in the last three decades of service in ministry. Sometimes I've been able to identify danger signs, and other times I've walked headlong into them, trying to believe the best. But through all this, the Lord has been growing wisdom in me and the desire to be one who can help bear others' burdens in a manner that is pure in heart.

Where in your ministry expression and personhood
do you need to mature and gain a heart of wisdom?

And where do you need to learn to walk beside others
with a quiet, non-anxious presence like Piglet?

Blessed are the peacemakers,
for they will be called
children of God.

Matthew 5 : 9

CHAPTER SEVEN

BLESSED
ARE THE PEACEMAKERS

Today we live in a society of echo chambers and cancel culture. If I do not agree with or like what you are saying, I simply annihilate you with my words or pretend that your voice, perspective, and very presence account for nothing.

On the other hand, if I like and agree with what you are saying, then we can be friends and perhaps even on "the same team" in our expressions of faith. This is a deeply troubling trend happening particularly in Christianity.

We are losing the art of relationships and the ability to engage in respectful conversations even where there are strong differing opinions. And more than that, we are engaging in very important discussions and dialogues in our society in a manner that is gravely adolescent. We need to grow up and stop being so defensive, reacting as though everything is a direct threat against our faith. That is quite simply not true.

When we look at the difference between the posture of a peacekeeper and a peacemaker, I think some much-needed clarification and adjustment can be achieved.

What comes to mind when you think of a peacekeeper? Perhaps the blue helmets and machine guns of the UN peacekeepers that I grew accustomed to while living in Sierra Leone, Guinea, and Liberia. Their very presence stated that peace was fragile and that civil or geopolitical unrest and crisis could happen at any moment. And it often did.

In war-torn countries around the globe, peace is short-lived and often tenuous in nature. The UN forces serve as both protective forces and reminders of that fragility.

Peacekeepers are on guard. They are armed and ready to enact their charge as soon as someone steps across the proverbial line. They engage as defenders, as ones who at a moment's notice will rise to defend their kingdom. This reminds me of the story in the Gospel of John where the Roman guards have come to take Jesus away to be tried under a corrupt government. Simon Peter, in a peacekeeping manner, drew his sword and cut off the ear of the high priest's servant.

In response, Jesus did the unthinkable. He picked up the bloody ear of the man who was going to take Him captive and with divine power attached it back to the man's head, leaving both the servant and Peter disoriented. You and I still get disoriented when our perception of what is righteous gets flipped on its head by the heart of Christ.

I have been in three riots in my life so far. One in New York City where police in full tactical gear were clearing out a park where squatters and homeless lived. Another in the nation of Guinea where political upheaval and an attempted coup was happening. And finally in the nation of The Gambia, West Africa, where a fourteen-year-old schoolboy was beaten to death by a schoolteacher who disciplined him. The nation went into a riot that I, along with several others from the missionary ship we were serving with, found ourselves in the middle of—with gunfire, cars being set on fire, and people being killed.

We were out in a remote village at the time, and as I lay down on my foam mattress on the floor of the team house, I pondered the chaos and destruction of the day's events while the sound of gunfire echoed around the area. Oddly, I was at perfect peace that night.

I wonder today, as we live in a climate of riotous reactions, how much wisdom we forfeit when we

> You and I still get disoriented when our perception of what is righteous gets flipped on its head by the heart of Christ.

back ourselves into a corner of being peacekeepers. In contrast, Jesus says, "Blessed are the peacemakers."

Peacemaking is a creative endeavor. It requires a posture of respectful curiosity. A desire to listen, engage, and at times negotiate. It requires maturity and the ability to see beyond the immediate.

As a child I have the distinct memory of watching the peace talks between Anwar Sadat of Egypt and Menachem Begin, Prime Minister of Israel. I did not understand all the complexities of the diplomatic protocols, but something inside me was fascinated. This was a very important process that was going to take time and effort.

Night after night the TV reports would tell of a pause in the talks over a point of disagreement or a hopeful step towards agreement, which would bring peace and stability to a region of the globe that has had its fair share of death and destruction. I remember the beaming smile of President Jimmy Carter and the triple handshake as the Camp David Peace Accord was signed on September 17, 1978. The world collectively breathed a sigh of relief.

Years into my adulthood, I would stand with the same fascination and respect when I stood silently in the sparse prison cell of Nelson Mandela on Robben Island, South Africa. And when I stood in President Ellen's oval office in Liberia and spoke with her of the war and genocide that had destroyed her country. And again, at a mural in Belfast, Northern Ireland, depicting Bloody Sunday.

We need peacemakers in our world today. You and I as followers of the Way are called to this.

Peacekeeping is defensive.

Peacemaking is creative.

Peacekeeping is self-preserving.

Peacemaking is invitational.

Peacekeeping seeks conformity to what it is.

Peacemaking contains hope for what could be.

Peacekeeping is weak.

Peacemaking requires meekness—great strength under total control.

Just like Peter, we seem to gravitate to using the sword. But Christ, in His loving-kindness, invites us to pick up the towel of serving. He invites us into partnership with the kingdom of God to bring peace—shalom in chaos. Chaos of geopolitical relations, chaos of marriage and family relations, chaos of creation systematically exploited. Chaos of folks hurt and betrayed by church authority gone unchecked, chaos of folks living without hope in this life and for the next.

But peacemaking is part of our inheritance
as the children of God.

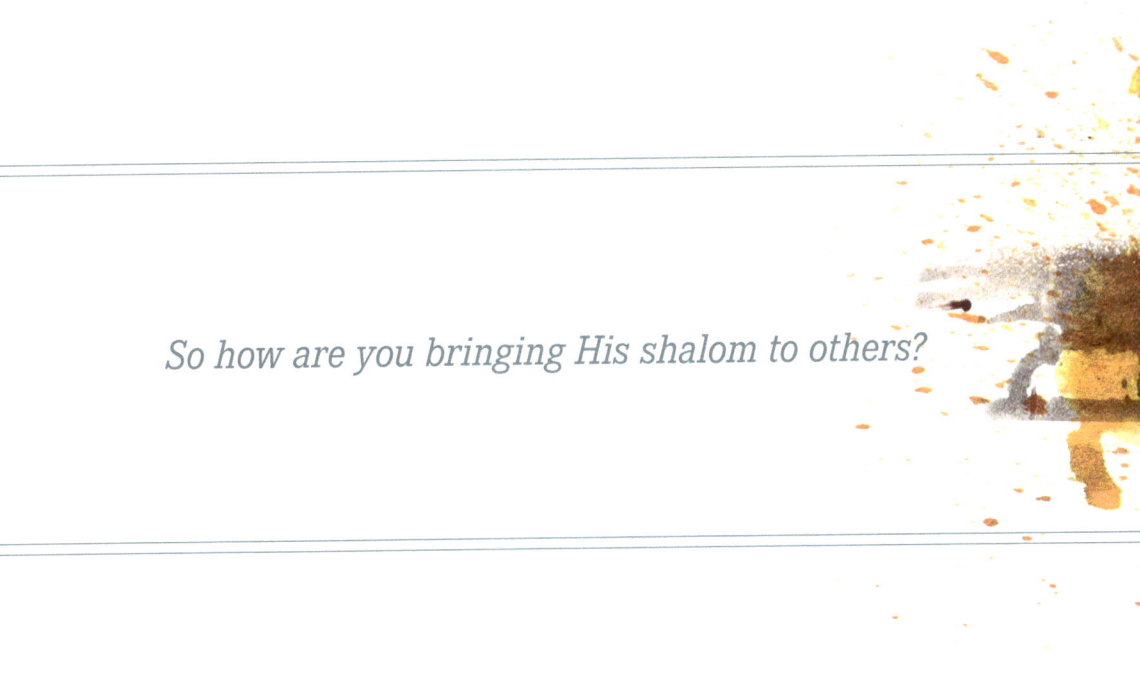

So how are you bringing His shalom to others?

Blessed are they that suffer persecution for justice' sake, for theirs is the kingdom of heaven.

Matthew 5: 10

CHAPTER EIGHT

BLESSED
ARE YOU WHEN
YOU ARE PERSECUTED

There is an epidemic happening in American Christian culture today, and it is contagious: taking offense. We seem to be growing increasingly fluent in this language. In doing so, we are becoming very aggressive in protection of our rights and seemingly circling the wagons to protect ourselves from the world around us.

It is becoming acceptable to scream louder, close the doors faster, get what you want first, and protect your way of life above all else. It's us against them. This is not a Christ-centered posture of living.

In taking this viewpoint, we are fueling the fires of prejudice, devaluing people, exploiting creation, and propagating anger that we have spiritualized and called righteous. We need to reorient ourselves around the gospel and live in the hope and kindness that our faith is founded on.

In society today we have been given the chance to criticize and even slander someone if we disagree with them. We relate to those who hold different views as hostile or worthless of time and care, and sometimes as people whose lives don't matter.

But the walls of our housing are decorated with scripture verses that seem to call us back to a Christ-postured life. Let's get those verses out of the picture frames and into our hearts!

The words Christ spoke challenge us and echo through eternity: "For I was hungry and you gave me something to eat, I was thirsty and you gave me something to drink, I was a stranger and you invited me in, I needed clothes and you clothed me, I was sick and you looked after me, I was in prison and you came to visit me" (Matt. 25:35–36).

> We need to reorient ourselves around the gospel and live in the hope and kindness that our faith is founded on.

We are grossly losing touch with the heart of the gospel. We sing songs about God loving us and being faithful to us in our churches but then walk out the doors with war paint on our faces and swords in our hands, ready to blast the next person or thought that seems to offend us.

We need to grow up. We need to learn to suffer well, with faithfulness and compassion.

As I have traveled the nations and experienced the global body of Christ, I am most struck and humbled by those who are genuinely experiencing true persecution for their faith. They seem to have a quiet assurance that their suffering is not in vain and that it is not theirs to seek vengeance, which belongs to the Lord.

I have stood in courtrooms in the developing world, where missionaries have been martyred, and borne witness to the gospel being extended to the accused by the family members of those who were murdered. I have watched a high court justice gasp at the profound and unexpected kindness shown in the light of confounding violence and murder. I have journeyed with family members as they seek to forgive and continue to choose life in the face of unspeakable loss.

We are not called to wage wars against culture and society. We are called to be beacons of hope in it, but too often we overlook the fruit of the Spirit—longsuffering.

Philippians 2:14-16 instructs us, "Do everything without grumbling or arguing, so that you may become blameless and pure, 'children of God without fault in a warped and crooked generation.' Then you will shine among them like stars in the sky as you hold firmly to the word of life."

So let's return our hearts, lives, actions, and investments back to the essence of the gospel for those who need to hear it—the good news of

Christ. You and I are as much in need of this hope as anyone else! Our society and culture are watching us. As followers of the Way, we are to shine light and point toward life.

The Beatitudes, in my opinion, are the most challenging words of Christ's teachings. They invite and even implore us to live in a way that is vastly different from the control and bondage of the leather of the empire. Instead, they call us into the life and freedom of the dirt of the kingdom of God.

It is in this dirt that we discover the power

of peace, joy, and righteousness.

This is the abundant life that Jesus offers us—the laying down

of our own rights and the taking on of His Spirit. So choose life,

that it may go well with you and your descendants.

BENEDICTION

As we consider all You have taught us and shown us,
God, we are humbled, and we are challenged.
Help us to allow these teachings to transform us,
long after we close the pages of this book.
May we carry with us the stories of those who have
embodied Your ways and Your heart and
allow their lives to impact how we live and love
in the places You've called us to and with the people
we encounter on our journey.

Father, we ask that your Son's teachings
would become our prayers . . .

Help us to be poor in spirit, that we may
encounter the kingdom of heaven.

Teach us to mourn and not be afraid to sit in the pain with You,
that we may be comforted.

May we hunger and thirst for righteousness, that we may be filled.

Help us to extend mercy freely, that we may be shown mercy.

Teach us to be pure in heart, that we may see You.

Show us how to be peacemakers, so we can be
called children of God.

And Father, should we face persecution for the sake of righteousness,
strengthen and sustain us—so we can experience Your kingdom.

Amen.

AMY BETH VELARDE

BETHANN MILLER

Bethann is the co-founder and owner of Safe Place, a ministry that provides support, training, care, and guidance to folks serving in Christ-centered ministry throughout the world. She is also a licensed chaplain and board-certified pastoral counselor.

Bethann began full-time ministry in 1995, first working in urban ministry and then going on to live and serve internationally for fourteen years. One of her deepest joys is caring for pastors, missionaries, and ministry leaders, and she has traveled to sixty-two nations to provide practical support, teaching, and pastoral care for them. The majority of Bethann's time is now spent supporting leadership teams and providing marriage intensives, debriefings, and personal and group retreats.

Bethann is married to Tom, who is a Licensed Professional Counselor specializing in marriage and family therapy. Bethann met Tom in Liberia, West Africa, where they were both serving as missionaries on a hospital ship.

In her free time, Bethann enjoys spending time with her two cats, watching the National Football League, riding a motorcycle named "Pearl," and relaxing with her husband and friends around their fire pit. They currently live in Lehigh Valley, PA, and actively serve in their local church.